So Many Sounds

by Ashlyn Adams

 HOUGHTON MIFFLIN HARCOURT
School Publishers

PHOTOGRAPHY CREDITS: Cover © Greenshoots Communications/Alamy; 1 © BananaStock/SuperStock; 2 © Blend Images/Alamy; 3 © Don Despain/Alamy; 4 © BananaStock/SuperStock; 5 © Richard Levine/Alamy; 6 © image100/Alamy; 7 © Sean Justice/Corbis; 8 © David Young-Wolff; 9 © Greenshoots Communications/Alamy; 10 © Curt Wiler/Alamy

Printed in China

ISBN-13: 978-0-547-42736-2
ISBN-10: 0-547-42736-0

5 6 7 8 0940 18 17 16 15 14 13 12
4500345273

There are lots of ways
to say things.
This girl talks.
She uses words to say,
"I'm hungry!"

This boy began to cry.
He uses loud sounds
and tears to say,
"I need my mother
or father!"

This girl laughs.
She uses a laugh
and a smile to say,
"I feel happy!"

These people clap
their hands together.
They use the sound
to say, "Good job!"

This woman rings a bell.
She uses the sound
of the bell to say,
"I am at your house."

This man whispers.
He uses a soft sound
and holds up
his finger to say,
"Shhh! Let's be quiet!"

This woman blows
a whistle.
She uses the sound
of the whistle to say,
"Stop! Nothing can move!"

This man beats a drum
again and again.
He uses the sound
of the drum to say,
"Come along to a dance!"

This man plays a flute.
He uses the sound
of the flute to say,
"I love you."
Sounds can say a lot!

Responding

Word Builder

What sounds do people make together?

Talk About It

Text to Text Think of other stories with people making sounds. What sounds did people make together? What did the sounds mean?

11

 **TARGET STRATEGY** **Monitor/Clarify**

Find ways to figure out what doesn't make sense.